Wishing you lots of Joy
Love, Health ~

DESSERT
Making it Rich Without Oil

HEALTHY RAW WHOLE FOOD TREATS

Dr. Ritamarie Loscalzo, MS, DC, CCN, DACBN
Chef Karen Osborne

FNF Publishing

Austin, Texas

Published in the United States of America

First Printing December 2010

Cover Design
Rosita Alvarez

Photography
Karen Osborne and Ryan Osborne

Book Design and Layout
Kristi Keenan

Editing and Formatting
Lauren Osborne

Disclaimer

The techniques and advice described in this book represent the opinions of the authors based on training and experience. The authors expressly disclaim any responsibility for any liability, loss or risk, personal or otherwise, which is incurred as a result of using any of the techniques, recipes or recommendations suggested herein. If in any doubt, or if requiring medical advice, please contact the appropriate health professional.

For other books and programs by Dr. Ritamarie and Chef Karen

Dr. Ritamarie's website: www.FreshnFunLiving.com

Chef Karen's Website: www.karenorawchef.com

DEDICATION

To our families and friends for their loving support during the long hours of recipe and content creation. Their willingness to taste test the recipes contributed greatly to the outcome.

To Scott and Scott, our partners in life with love and kisses.

To Ryan, Lauren, Eric and Kevin, our children. Thanks. We love you.

Karen Ritamarie

Karen and Ritamarie
December 2010

FOREWORD

When Karen first suggested we co-author a book about creating decadent nutritious desserts, I was excited by the prospect. Karen has a talent for taking simple, ordinary foods and magically transforming them into elegant, healthy and delicious desserts. The pictures on the cover and throughout demonstrate that talent. Working with Karen is a dream. She puts her all into everything she does, is meticulous about details and, as we discovered throughout this project, she has an up-'til-now hidden talent for food photography!

You couldn't ask for a better co-author. She took my recipes, tested them, tweaked them, photographed them and added them to her own to create this masterpiece. There is no other dessert book quite like this one.

The desserts in traditional recipe books are filled with sugar, processed flour, trans and oxidized fats (the kind that damage your arteries and impede your immune system), dairy products and other undesirable ingredients.

Even the gluten-free and vegan "healthy" alternatives left us flat. Many of the recipes are just too complicated for the average busy person to make on a regular basis. Still others are loaded with oil and so-called "healthy" alternative sweeteners.

What we've created is a book of dessert recipes using only whole, raw, plant based ingredients. There's no oil, no honey, no agave, no gluten, no dairy. We sweeten with whole foods and make it rich with whole food fats like nuts, seeds, avocado and coconut. We even slip in vegetables whenever we can.

This is truly a unique book and I am proud to be the co-author with the amazing Karen Osborne.

With deep gratitude and love,

Dr. Ritamarie Loscalzo, MS, DC, CCN, DACBN

ACKNOWLEDGEMENTS

A book like this just wouldn't be possible without the help and inspiration of many people.

Special thanks is extended to our teachers, near and far, living and passed who inspired, motivated and encouraged us to be our best. The knowledge and experience you've imparted to us has contributed to who we are today.

To our students whose expressions of delight when they "get it" make all the time and effort worth every minute. We learn as much from you as you from us. We thank you from the bottom of our hearts.

To Rosita Alvarez, our graphic artist. We so appreciate your ability to take the vague notions in our heads and transform them into art that reflects the love we put into our creations.

Special appreciation to Lauren Osborne, who painstakingly formatted the recipes into a beautiful manuscript, and corrected our spelling and grammar at the same time.

To the Scotts, Scott Osborne, and Scott Claver, our dear partners in life, who allow us the space to concoct edible wonders and to create books and classes so we can teach and share them with others.

And finally, we appreciate our children. They've tasted our creations over the years and taught us so much in the process. Thanks Eric and Kevin, Ritamarie's sons and Lauren and Ryan, Karen's daughters. Our lives would not be complete without you.

INTRODUCTION

The Art of Dessert Making

Imagine how much better your world would be if people in it felt better! When you feel good, you feel rich, regardless of how much money you have in the bank or how much gold and jewels you've accumulated. When you feel uncomfortable in your body, nagged by symptoms like pain, inflammation, brain fog, fatigue and a host of other complaints, all the riches in the world can't make up for your bodily suffering.

More and more, science is showing us the intimate connection between what you put in your mouth and how you feel! The time is right for changing the quality and quantity of food you consume so you can feel at your best and are unstoppable.

Just about everyone loves good desserts. Desserts make your tongue feel gleeful and your heart sing. But have you ever thought about how your favorite desserts ultimately affect your body? Most of our best loved desserts contain gluten, dairy, unhealthy trans fats and refined sugar.

Standard desserts are full of ingredients that cause people to age prematurely and develop many health problems including inflammatory bowel diseases like Crohn's and ulcerative colitis, irritable bowel, asthma, ear infections, sinus congestion, eczema, autistic spectrum disorders, attention deficit hyperactivity disorder, autoimmune disorders, hormone imbalances and sensory integration disorder.

So What's Really in Your Favorite Desserts?

The list of ingredients in your favorite desserts can be scary. Here's the low-down on the most common ingredients in just about every dessert on the planet.

All Purpose Flour is made from wheat, which has been refined by removing the outer layer of bran and germ, where most of the nutrients are found. About 20 minerals and 8 vitamins are removed from the wheat during processing. When it's enriched, only 5 of these 28 nutrients are then put back. The nutrients that are put back are synthetically-derived, chemical vitamins, rather than the natural forms in the original grain.

When you eat refined flour, aka white flour, your body fails to get the nutrients that are naturally present in whole grains. Also, your body's stores of these nutrients are depleted, especially the B vitamins, which give you energy and help you think and learn.

The flour used in dessert making is usually made from wheat, unless it's explicitly stated that it's wheat or gluten free. Gluten has been linked to many serious health challenges, including autoimmune conditions, depression, psychosis, ADD and autism and it's estimated that over 30% of people are intolerant to it, meaning that your body creates antibodies that attack it when eaten. For details on how gluten can affect your body, visit www.drritamarie.com/glutenfree and download a free packet of materials.

Butter is the fat from cow's milk. It's high in cholesterol and saturated fats and contains traces of the hormones fed to the cows to stimulate milk production. Excess consumption has been shown to contribute to heart disease and some forms of cancer.

Margarine is a fat made by chemically altering vegetable oils to make them solid at room temperature. Many people consider margarine to be a health food and freely substitute it for butter thinking they are doing their body good. Studies over the past 20 years have shown that margarine is actually more harmful than butter, because processing creates a type of fat known as trans fat which damages your blood vessels, stimulates your liver to produce cholesterol and causes damage to your cells that can lead to cancer.

Refined sugar consumption has been linked to many health problems. A few of these include diabetes, dental cavities, heart disease, hyperactivity, inability to concentrate, osteoporosis and acne. Sugar decreases the activity of your infection-fighting white blood cells, called macrophages, by 50%, so eating it can lead to more frequent colds, flu and other infectious diseases and even cancer. It also depletes the body of B-vitamins resulting in a reduced tolerance for stress and other imbalances.

Eggs are high in cholesterol and hormone residues, and an inflammatory fat called arachidonic acid. Excess consumption has been associated with heart disease. They are also among the top six most common allergy foods.

Chocolate is everyone's favorite. It's been getting a lot of press for its health benefits over the past few years. In spite of the fact that there are indeed some positive nutritional benefits in chocolate, many people react adversely. It's said that raw chocolate is better than chocolate made after the cacao beans have been roasted. This certainly appears to be true; still, I've worked with quite a number of people who get very agitated from eating chocolate, even raw chocolate. We have omitted chocolate from all of our recipes and substituted carob instead. If you are a chocolate fan, you may substitute chocolate for carob in any recipe as long as you remember to sweeten to taste. Carob is naturally sweet and chocolate is naturally bitter.

Soy is not in and of itself a problem and many people eat it for its hormone protective effects. The big problem with soy is that a lot of people are allergic to it. It's listed among the top six most common food allergens. Soy also contains glutamate, an excitatory neurotransmitter, and in excess, can contribute to attention issues and focusing difficulties, especially in children. We've opted to make all of our recipes soy free to respect those who are sensitive. While moderate quantities of soy may indeed offer health enhancing effects, regular consumption of large quantities of soy can affect your hormones.

Creating Nutritious and Delicious Desserts

When making a transition from the standard American diet to a more health supportive one, many people ask "But what about dessert? Do I need to give it up altogether, or can I sometimes 'cheat'?" The answer is that you can have delicious desserts without 'cheating'. In fact, you can learn to make desserts that are so nutritious you can eat them for breakfast. Most people can indulge in healthfully prepared and delicious living foods vegan treats without compromising their health. That said, desserts should never comprise a significant portion of anyone's diet, no matter how healthfully prepared. We believe that greens should be the cornerstone of a healthy diet.

A first step towards achieving better health and feeling better is likely to be finding healthy versions of your favorite 'junk' food and sweet desserts.

Most any type of dessert can be made using whole, gluten-free, dairy-free and sugar free ingredients. It's easy to make cakes, pies, cookies, ice creams, candies, and puddings, to name but a few. The desserts in this book combine nuts, seeds, fruits, both fresh and dried, coconut and vegetables and leave out the white flour, sugar, shortening, butter, eggs and oils found in conventional recipes.

Dessert can be as simple as chopping apples and sprinkling them with cinnamon or as elaborate as a masterpiece cheese cake. Even a simple bowl of fresh ripe berries makes a delicious dessert.

The recipes in this book fall into the following categories:

- Cookies, Bars and Brownies
- Pies and Tarts
- Cake
- Candy
- Frozen Concoctions
- Other Fun Foods
- Toppings and Components

No matter what your diet, vegan, vegetarian, omnivore or carnivore, if you eat fresh fruits and veggies and lots of greens with your other stuff, you are going to be healthier and feel better. Eating our whole food desserts is a great way to increase the amount of nutritious food you put into your body and decrease the amount of toxic food with little change in habit or pleasure. The end result just may be a flat comfortable belly, a clear mind and an energetic body - all this, while enjoying delicious food.

Many, if not most, of the recipes in other raw vegan dessert books are high in oil and sweeteners. Many of them are quite delicious but a lot of them are too complicated and time consuming to make on a regular basis. There are also a lot of recipes that are simple and easy and taste pretty good, but pretty good is usually not enough to satisfy your craving for comfort foods.

We're here to teach you the art of creating elegant, delicious desserts that are quick, easy and fun to prepare. They're made using whole foods (even the sweeteners) with no added oils. Whole foods are a complete package – containing everything your body needs to fully utilize all the nutrients contained within.

Glossary of Special Ingredients Used in this Book

What follows is a list of some of the "not so common" items that when added to your culinary vocabulary will take your desserts to the next level. Once you try them, you'll see how easy they are to use.

Coconut Butter (Artisana is our favorite brand) is raw and organic pureed coconut. It's made from the whole coconut flesh not just the oil. Therefore, it gives you the whole food nutrition of the oil, fiber, protein, vitamins and minerals. It's high in manganese and a good source of essential amino acids and copper. It's a naturally saturated fat containing medium-chain fatty acids that your body can metabolize efficiently. Once chilled, it solidifies, helping to create a firm consistency in the dessert. It's a key ingredient in cheese cake, pumpkin pie and other desserts that need to "stand up". It's available at many health foods stores and online at http://www.premierorganics.org

Young Thai Coconuts can be purchased at Asian markets and many natural food stores. They contain a lightly sweet water that's a great source of electrolytes. The flesh is soft and creamy, in contrast to that of the mature coconuts that are more commonly found in supermarkets. The young coconuts are much easier to open than the mature ones and can be used in making creamy desserts. The coconut meat can be blended with the coconut water to make a custard like cream.

Dried Fruits and Dates contain pectin, a natural gelling agent, and can be used as binders and whole food sweeteners at the same time. In some recipes they are used whole and dry. In others, they are soaked first and in still others, they are made into a paste and added in measured amounts, similar to liquid sweeteners like honey and maple syrup. The advantage of using dried fruits as sweeteners is that you get a whole food nutrient bundle, rather than just sweetness.

Sunflower Lecithin can be used to bind fats and liquids keeping them from separating in your dessert. This will help your pie keep its shape and texture. Sunflower lecithin is a great alternative to soy lecithin for people avoiding soy and is available from Love Raw Foods. It can be purchased online from http://www.bluemountainorganics.com

Psyllium is a plant-derived soluble fiber available as husks or powder. It absorbs liquid and will thicken your dessert and help it hold its shape. As a side benefit, it's also a good intestinal lubricant. In our travels, we've discovered that the powder is easier to find than the husks. As a result, we've written all the recipes using powder. If you're using the husks, you'll probably need more than the measurement that is written.

Coconut Nectar is the sap from the blossoms of the coconut tree. It's a low glycemic sweetener, meaning it doesn't cause a spike in blood sugar shortly after being consumed. It provides minerals, amino acids, vitamin C and B vitamins. The sap is evaporated at low temperatures to remove excess moisture and thicken it. This is a relatively new product on the market. We use it very sparingly, only when whole food sweeteners like dates and raisins would not provide the texture we required by a particular recipe. It can be purchased online at http://www.coconutsecret.com

Chia seeds are a good source of omega - 3 fatty acids, which protect your heart, enhance your immune system and provide natural anti-inflammatory support to joints and other body parts. They're also a good source of fiber, calcium, phosphorus, and manganese. Chia seeds make a good binder when ground in a high speed blender or a coffee grinder and then added to recipes. They can also be used to create delicious, easy-to-make pudding when soaked in water, fresh juice or nut milk and then flavored. The ideal ratio of chia seeds to water when soaking is 1:5. Chia seeds have become quite popular and are now available at most health food stores and even some supermarkets. You can purchase them more economically in bulk online at http://www.drritamarie.com/go/chiaseed

Lucuma powder is made from the dried fruit of lucuma, a Peruvian fruit that's been honored since the time of the Incas. The powder has a maple-like flavor and is an excellent source of fiber, vitamins, and minerals, especially beta carotene, niacin, and iron. It is available at many health food stores and online at http://www.drritamarie.com/go/lucuma

Mesquite powder is a low glycemic whole food sweetener made by grinding the edible bean-like pods of South American mesquite shrubs. It has a smoky sweet flavor similar to caramel and is an excellent source of protein, the amino acid lysine, calcium, magnesium, potassium, iron and zinc. It's available online at http://www.drritamarie.com/go/mesquite

Vanilla Powder aka Ground Vanilla Beans This is simply vanilla beans that have been ground to a fine powder. It's dark brown in color, just like the whole vanilla bean pods. When a recipe would normally call for vanilla extract, we use ground vanilla beans to be sure we are not getting any gluten, alcohol or glycerin. You may substitute vanilla extract for the ground vanilla beans in any recipe. Be sure to get the kind that has no added sugar or preservatives. There are several organic brands available at most health food stores. The vanilla powder, aka ground vanilla beans can be purchased online at http://www.ultimatesuperfoods.com

Irish moss is a sea vegetable that's a good binder, thickener and gelling agent. It's a great source of nutrients such as sulfur compounds, protein, iodine, bromine, beta-carotene, calcium, iron, magnesium, manganese, zinc, phosphorus, potassium, selenium, pectin, B vitamins and vitamin C. The kind we use in our recipes has been sundried and sun bleached and is a light beige color. There's a recipe for Irish moss gel in the last chapter. Irish Moss is available online at http://www.drritamarie.com/go/irishmoss

Choosing Ingredients and Getting Started
Deliciously Nutritious Whole Foods Raw Desserts

The chart on the next page contains a listing of many of the whole foods that can be used in making desserts. Many of them are used in our recipes. The extras have been listed to give you ideas for substitutions.

The first time you make a recipe, do it as we suggest. Once you get a feel for how the recipe turns out, feel free to substitute one fruit or nut for another, add or change spices and seasonings, or combine several recipe components to create your own unique masterpiece.

The wonderful thing about making raw desserts is that it's not rocket science. When you make angel food cake, meringue or any of a variety of traditional desserts, you need to pay careful attention to measurements and timing. Not so with living foods. There is a lot of wiggle room.

Have fun with all of this, and enjoy the recipes. Your body will love you for taking such good care of it and reward you with abundant energy, mental clarity and joy!

Share your masterpieces at www.wholefoodrawdesserts.com

WHOLE FOOD DESSERT INGREDIENT OPTIONS

Nuts	Fresh & Frozen Fruits	Herbs & Spices
Macadamia	Strawberries	Cinnamon
Cashews	Blueberries	Cardamom
Almonds	Raspberries	Nutmeg
Hazelnuts	Blackberries	Coriander
Pecans	Cherries	Clove
Walnuts	Mangoes	Fennel
Pine Nuts	Peaches	Mint
Pistachios	Bananas	Ginger
Brazil Nuts	Pineapple	
Coconuts	Persimmon	**Thickeners/Binders**
	Papaya	Psyllium Husks
Seeds	Apples	Agar
Pumpkin	Oranges	Kudzu
Sesame	Kiwi	Arrowroot
Flax	Pears	Avocado
Hemp	Pomegranate	Irish Moss
Sunflower	Lemon	Flax Seed
Chia Seeds	Lime	Chia Seeds
Nut Seed Butters	**Dried Fruits**	**Sweeteners**
Almond	Dates	Stevia
Cashew	Figs	Pureed Dried Fruit
Coconut	Raisins	Yacon Powder
Sesame (tahini)	Dried Apricots	Lucuma Powder
Pumpkin Seed	Goji Berries	Mesquite Powder
Hemp Seed	Yacon Slices	Coconut Nectar
Macadamia		
	Freeze-Dried Fruit Powders blueberry, pomegranate, cherry, strawberry, blackberry, mixed berry, mango	
Flavorings		
Carob		
Vanilla (whole bean or powder)		
Extracts - Mint, Orange, Lemon, Maple, Almond, Vanilla		

Suggested Equipment...for Creating Delicious Desserts

 Food Processor This is a vital piece of equipment if you plan to make a lot of living foods recipes. It's used for making pie crusts, cakes, cookies and crackers and for chopping and grating ingredients. We recommend you get a large capacity food processor, 14 cups or greater, to most efficiently process your recipes. Reliable and sturdy are the Hamilton Beach Big Mouth and the Cuisinart 14 cup or higher. Available at kitchen stores and discount chains.

 A good quality blender For best results, invest in a high speed blender, like Vitamix, Blendtec or the sturdier of the consumer models available at local stores. You'll use it whenever a recipe calls for a smooth consistency component, as for custards, smoothies, purees and toppings.

http://www.drritamarie.com/go/Vitamix

http://www.drritamarie.com/go/Blendtec

 Dehydrator Choose a dehydrator that has a temperature control dial and removable shelves so you can fit pie crusts inside.

http://www.DrRitamarie.com/go/excalibur

 Citrus Squeezer Many of our recipes call for lemon or lime juice. You can use a simple hand squeezer, an electric juicer or a fork.

http://www.DrRitamarie.com/go/CitrusSqueezer

http://www.DrRitamarie.com/go/CitrusJuicer

 Also available at supermarkets, kitchen supply stores and superstores like Target.

Microplane These come in a variety of sizes and are useful for zesting fruit peels and creating the powdered sugar effect on the top of desserts using nuts and seeds.

http://www.DrRitamarie.com/go/Microplaner

Spring-form Pans

http://www.DrRitamarie.com/go/SpringformPan

These pans are ideal for making cheesecakes and other desserts that "stand up". The sides release for easy unmolding of your cake from the pan. They can also be used to shape layer cakes.

Tart Pans The bottoms pop out of these pans, making them ideal for creating tarts. They are also called cheesecake pans. They make it easy to remove pies and tarts from the pan and onto your plate. They come in a variety of sizes, including mini tarts and cup-cake tins.

http://www.drritamarie.com/go/minitartpans

http://www.drritamarie.com/go/tartpan

http://www.drritamarie.com/go/minicheesecakepan

Nut Milk Bag These are fine mesh bags with a draw string at the top. They are used for straining pulp when making nut milk.

http://www.drritamarie.com/go/nutmilkbag

Glass or metal pans in a variety of sizes. It's great to have a variety of sizes yet in reality just one or two will do. It depends on how elaborate you choose to get. We suggest an 8x8 square pan, a loaf pan and a couple of pie pans.

Parchment paper, wax paper or saran wrap

CHAPTER 1
Cookies, Bars & Brownies

"Oatmeal" Raisin Cookie Bars

Superfood Brownies

Cinnamon Buckwheat Crispy Cookies

Vanilla Mint Crisps

Rocky Road Brownies

S'mores

Turtle Brownies

Superfood Energy Bars

"OATMEAL" RAISIN COOKIE BARS

Yield: 8X8 pan - These have the flavor of the old comfort food, but supply you with plenty of energy.

INGREDIENTS

- 1 cup unsweetened finely shredded dried coconut
- 1 cup almonds, preferably soaked and dehydrated
- 1/4 teaspoon salt
- 1/4 cup lucuma powder
- 1/4 cup mesquite powder
- 1/2 teaspoon ground vanilla beans or vanilla extract
- 1 teaspoon cinnamon
- 16 pitted Medjool dates
- 1/2 cup raisins

DIRECTIONS

1. Process the coconut, almonds and salt in a food processor until finely ground.
2. Add the lucuma powder, mesquite powder, vanilla and cinnamon.
3. Process the mixture until combined.
4. With the food processor running, add the dates a few at a time.
5. Process just until the mixture begins to stick together.
6. Pour the mixture into an 8X8 glass pan and gently stir in the raisins.
7. Firmly press the mixture into the pan.
8. Chill for at least 2 hours, slice and enjoy!

"Oatmeal" Raisin Cookie Bars

Superfood Brownies

SUPERFOOD BROWNIES

Yield: 8X8 pan - The combination of vanilla and carob makes a delicious chocolate-like brownie. The kale is not detectible and it helps your body absorb the sugar from the dates.

INGREDIENTS

- 2 cups de-stemmed Kale, lightly packed
- 1/8 - 1/4 teaspoon salt
- 2 cups walnuts, preferably soaked and dehydrated
- 1 cup pecans, preferably soaked and dehydrated
- 1 tablespoon ground vanilla beans or vanilla extract
- 1 1/2 cups pitted Medjool dates
- 2/3 cup carob powder
- 2 teaspoons water

DIRECTIONS

1. Process the kale and salt in a food processor until chopped.
2. Remove the kale to a bowl and set aside.
3. Process the walnuts, pecans and vanilla until finely ground being careful not to over process into a nut butter.
4. Add the dates and kale and process until the mixture begins to stick together.
5. Add the carob powder and process until it is incorporated.
6. Add the water and pulse a few times.
7. Press into an 8 X 8 glass pan and chill for at least an hour.
8. Slice and serve.

CINNAMON BUCKWHEAT CRISPY COOKIES

Yield: 1 dehydrator tray - Crispy and crunchy, these simple low glycemic cookies really satisfy!

INGREDIENTS

- 1 cup buckwheat, soaked and sprouted (See instructions in Chapter 7)
- 1/4 cup coconut nectar
- 1/8 teaspoon salt
- 1 teaspoon ground vanilla beans or vanilla extract
- 2 teaspoons cinnamon
- 2 drops orange essential oil

DIRECTIONS

1. Process all ingredients until smooth in a food processor fitted with the S blade.
2. Spread thin on a non stick dehydrator sheet.
3. Dehydrate at 105 for 2 hours.
4. Score* into desired size cookies.
5. Continue dehydrating for 3 more hours.
6. Flip the tray and remove the non stick sheet.
7. Continue dehydrating for 18 more hours or until crispy. Dehydration time will vary due to the humidity in the air.

* To score, make shallow cuts in the surface of the batter so that it will easily break apart into the desired size and shape when dry. It works best to press down through the mixture with a pizza rocker, but a knife can be used as well.

Cinnamon Buckwheat Crispy Cookies

Vanilla Mint Crisps

VANILLA MINT CRISPS

Yield: 1 deydratpr tray. This is a delicious, light, refreshing crispy treat. Add 2 teaspoons of carob powder for a carob mint cookie.

INGREDIENTS

- 1 cup buckwheat, soaked and sprouted (See instructions in Chapter 7)
- 1/4 cup coconut nectar
- 1/8 teaspoon salt
- 1 teaspoon ground vanilla beans or vanilla extract
- 2 drops peppermint essential oil

DIRECTIONS

1. Process all the ingredients in a food processor fitted with the S blade.
2. Spread thin on a non stick dehydrator sheet.
3. Dehydrate at 105 for 2 hours.
4. Score* into desired shapes and sizes.
5. Continue dehydrating for 3 more hours.
6. Flip the tray and remove the non stick sheet.
7. Continue dehydrating 18 more hours or until crispy.
8. Store in an airtight container in the freezer.

* To score, make shallow cuts in the surface of the batter so that it will easily break apart into the desired size and shape when dry. It works best to press down through the mixture with a pizza rocker, but a knife can be used as well.

ROCKY ROAD BROWNIES

Yield: Twenty four 2" sq. brownies. This is a lighter brownie using fruit as a base instead of nuts. The marshmallow is a fun and nutritious addition.

INGREDIENTS

- 3 cups pitted Medjool dates
- 1 1/2 cup dried black mission figs
- 2 teaspoons ground vanilla beans or vanilla extract
- 1/4 teaspoon salt
- 3/4 cup lucuma powder
- 1 cup pecans, chopped
- 6 tablespoons carob powder
- 1 recipe Marshmallow Topping (recipe in Chapter 7)
- 1 recipe Carob Topping (recipe in Chapter 7)

DIRECTIONS

1. Line an 8x12 cookie sheet with parchment paper.
2. Pulse the dates, figs, vanilla and salt in a food processor and process until the dates and figs are chopped.
3. Add the lucuma powder and carob powder and process until combined.
4. Roughly chop the pecans and spread them onto the cookie sheet.
5. Press the dough on top of the pecans into the cookie sheet.
6. Chill the brownie layer for 4 hours.
7. Remove the brownies from the cookie sheet by pulling up the parchment paper. Flip the brownies so that the nuts are on top and slice.
8. Chill the brownies while preparing the marshmallow topping.
9. Put the marshmallow mixture in a pastry bag and pipe on top of the brownies.
10. Chill while preparing the carob topping.
11. Put the carob mixture in a pastry bag and pipe on top of the marshmallow layer.

Notes: If you don't have a pastry bag, you can either cut the corner off of a zip lock bag and pipe the toppings on that way or spoon the marshmallow topping on each square and drizzle carob topping on with a spoon.

Rocky Road Brownies

S'mores

S'MORES

Yield: 8" X 8" pan. The apricots, walnuts and lucuma combine to give the base a "graham cracker" flavor.

INGREDIENTS

- 1/2 cup walnuts, preferably soaked and dehydrated
- 1/2 cup almonds, preferably soaked and dehydrated
- 1/2 teaspoon ground vanilla beans or vanilla extract
- 1/4 teaspoon salt
- 1/2 cup finely shredded unsweetened dried coconut
- 3/4 cup dried Turkish apricots
- 1 cup pitted Medjool dates
- 1/2 cup lucuma powder
- 1 tablespoon water, if needed to hold mixture together
- 1 recipe Marshmallow Topping (recipe in Chapter 7)
- 1 recipe Carob Topping (recipe in Chapter 7)

DIRECTIONS

1. Process all of the ingredients except the lucuma powder, water and the toppings in a food processor until chopped and the mixture begins to stick together.
2. Add the lucuma powder, and process until incorporated and the mixture begins to stick together again. Add water only if needed for mixture to hold together.
3. Firmly press the mixture into a parchment lined (optional) 8 X 8 glass pan.
4. Chill for at least 4 hours.
5. If it is lined with parchment, remove the mixture from the pan by pulling up the parchment.
6. Slice into 2" squares.
7. Put the marshmallow topping in a pastry bag and pipe topping onto each square. Chill the squares while you prepare the carob topping.
8. Put the carob topping in a pastry bag and pipe on top of the marshmallow.
9. Chill the s'mores for at least 1 hour and serve.

Notes: If you don't have a pastry bag, you can either cut the corner off of a zip lock bag and pipe the toppings on that way or spoon the caramel topping on each square and drizzle carob topping on with a spoon.

TURTLE BROWNIES

Yield: Twenty four 2" squares -The creamy caramel topping makes this a luscious treat.

INGREDIENTS

- 3 cups pitted Medjool dates
- 1 1/2 cups dried black mission figs
- 2 teaspoons ground vanilla beans or vanilla extract
- 1/4 teaspoon salt
- 3/4 cup lucuma powder
- 6 tablespoons carob powder
- 1 cup pecans, chopped
- 1 recipe Caramel Topping (recipe in Chapter 7)
- 1 recipe Carob Topping (recipe in Chapter 7)

DIRECTIONS

1. Line an 8" x 12" cookie sheet with parchment paper.
2. Pulse the dates, figs, vanilla and salt in food processor and process until the dates and figs are chopped.
3. Add the lucuma powder and carob powder and process until combined.
4. Roughly chop the pecans and spread them on the cookie sheet.
5. Press the dough on top of the pecans in the cookie sheet and chill for 4 hours.
6. Remove from the sheet by pulling up the parchment paper. Flip so the nuts are on top and slice.
7. Make Caramel Topping.
8. Put the Caramel Topping in a pastry bag and chill for at least 2 hours.
9. Pipe on top of the brownies.
10. Chill the brownies while preparing the carob topping.
11. Put the Carob Topping in a pastry bag and pipe on top of the caramel layer.
12. Chill the brownies for at least 1 hour and serve.

Notes: If you don't have a pastry bag, you can either cut the corner off of a zip lock bag and pipe the toppings on that way or spoon the caramel topping on each square and drizzle carob topping on with a spoon.

Turtle Brownies

Superfood Energy Bars

SUPERFOOD ENERGY BARS

Yield: 8 X 8 pan. These great tasting bars are loaded with protein, omega 3s, selenium and zinc and taste like malted brownies.

INGREDIENTS

- 1/2 cup raisins
- 1/2 cup dates
- 1/2 cup water
- 1 1/2 cups walnuts
- 1/2 cup Brazil nuts
- 1/4 teaspoon salt
- 2 tablespoons maca powder
- 1 teaspoon ground vanilla beans or vanilla extract
- 2 tablespoons carob powder
- 1 teaspoon psyllium powder
- 1/2 cup chia seeds, ground
- 1/4 cup hemp seeds
- 1/4 cup pumpkin seeds
- 1/4 cup goji berries

DIRECTIONS

1. Make a paste by blending the dates, raisins and water in a high speed blender until smooth. Set this aside.
2. Process the walnuts, Brazil nuts, salt, maca, vanilla, carob powder, psyllium powder and chia seeds in a food processor until the nuts are finely ground.
3. Add the date and raisin paste and continue to process until the mixture makes a dough.
4. Add the hemp seeds, pumpkin seeds and goji berries, and pulse briefly to mix.
5. Spread the mixture into an 8 X 8 glass pan lined with saran wrap or parchment paper. .
6. Let it sit for 10 minutes.
7. Remove from glass pan and slice into desired sizes.
8. Place brownies on a dehydrator tray lined with a mesh screen and dehydrate at 105° F for 8 hours or more to taste. Alternatively, you can place them in a glass dish and freeze them for several hours for a chewier energy bar.

CHAPTER 2

Pies & Tarts

Blueberry Lemon "Poppyseed" Tart

Banana Coconut Cream Pie

"Key Lime" Pie

Carob Mint Pie

Mango Coconut Fruit Tart

Orange Carob Pudding Pie

Peach Mango Pie

Strawberry Banana Coconut Cream Pie

Nut Free Pie Crust

Simple Nut Free Pie Crust

Blueberry Lemon "Poppyseed" Tart

BLUEBERRY LEMON "POPPYSEED" TART

Yield: 6" tart pan - This is a delicious berry tart bursting with juicy flavor. It can also be made in a 9" pan for a thinner tart.

INGREDIENTS

- 1 cup finely shredded unsweetened dried coconut
- 1/8 teaspoon salt
- 1/2 cup almonds, preferably soaked and dehydrated
- 1 teaspoon psyllium powder
- 1 teaspoon ground vanilla beans or vanilla extract
- 1 teaspoon lemon zest
- 8 pitted Medjool dates
- 1/2 cup peeled zucchini puree (about 1 zucchini)
- 2 tablespoons whole chia seeds
- 1 recipe Blueberry Jam (recipe in Chapter 7)
- 1 recipe Vanilla Custard (recipe in Chapter 7)
- 1 1/2 – 2 cups fresh blueberries (or a 10 ounce bag of frozen)

DIRECTIONS

1. Process the coconut, salt and almonds in a food processor until finely ground.
2. Add the psyllium, vanilla and lemon zest, and process until incorporated.
3. With the food processor running, add the dates and process until mixed.
4. Add the peeled zucchini puree and the chia seeds, and process until combined into a dough.
5. Press the dough into the bottom of a 6" tart pan.
6. Spread the Blueberry Jam on top of the cake base and chill while preparing the Vanilla Custard.
7. Spread the Vanilla Custard on top of the jam layer.
8. Top with fresh blueberries.
9. Chill for at least 2 hours.

BANANA COCONUT CREAM PIE

Yield: 9" Pie. This creamy and delicious pie is a big hit.

INGREDIENTS - CRUST

- 1 cup almonds, preferably soaked and dehydrated
- 1 cup finely shredded unsweetened dried coconut
- 1/4 teaspoon salt
- 1/2 cup pecans, preferably soaked and dehydrated
- 1/2 cup pitted Medjool dates

INGREDIENTS - FILLING

- 5 bananas
- 1/2 cup coconut butter
- 1/2 cup water
- 4 pitted Medjool dates
- 1 teaspoon ground vanilla beans or vanilla extract
- 1/8 teaspoon salt
- 1 teaspoon sunflower lecithin
- Banana slices, ground vanilla beans and dried coconut to decorate top

DIRECTIONS - CRUST

1. Process the almonds, coconut and salt in a food processor until finely ground.
2. Add the pecans and process just until they are chopped.
3. Add the dates and process until mixture begins to stick together.
4. Press the crust mixture into a glass pie dish.

DIRECTIONS - FILLING

1. Slice 4 bananas and place them in a bowl.
2. Blend 1 banana, coconut butter, water, dates, vanilla and salt until smooth.
3. Add the lecithin and blend until it is incorporated.
4. Pour the mixture over the sliced bananas and stir well.
5. Spread the filling in the pie crust and decorate as desired with coconut, vanilla and banana slices. Chill and serve.

Banana Coconut Cream Pie

"Key Lime" Pie

"KEY LIME" PIE

Yield: 9" pie - Although key lime pie is not actually green, the spinach gives this pie the nice color that has come to be associated with key lime pie and some extra nutrients to help process the sugars in the pie.

INGREDIENTS - CRUST

- 1 cup almonds, ground, preferably soaked and dehydrated
- 1 cup finely shredded unsweetened dried coconut
- 1/4 teaspoon salt
- 1/2 cup pecans, preferably soaked and dehydrated
- 1/2 cup pitted Medjool dates

INGREDIENTS - FILLING

- 1/2 cup lime juice
- 1 cup spinach
- 1 banana
- 1/2 cup coconut butter
- 6 pitted Medjool dates
- 1/2 teaspoon vanilla powder or vanilla extract
- 1/8 teaspoon salt
- 1 teaspoon sunflower lecithin

DIRECTIONS - CRUST

1. Process the almonds, coconut and salt in a food processor until finely ground.
2. Add the pecans and process until they are coarsely chopped.
3. Add the dates and process until the mixture begins to stick together.
4. Press the crust mixture into a glass pie dish.

DIRECTIONS - FILLING

1. Blend the lime juice, spinach, banana, coconut butter, dates, vanilla and salt in a high speed blender until smooth.
2. Add the lecithin and blend until it is incorporated.
3. Pour filling mixture into the pie crust and chill for at least 4 hours.

CAROB MINT PIE

Yield: 9" pie - The carob and the mint make this a cool and refreshing treat.

INGREDIENTS - CRUST

- 1 cup almonds, preferably soaked and dehydrated
- 1 cup finely shredded dried coconut
- 1/4 teaspoon salt
- 1 cup pitted Medjool dates

INGREDIENTS - FILLING

- 1/2 cup Irish moss paste (recipe in Chapter 7)
- 2 cups pitted Medjool dates, soaked in water for 20 minutes
- 1/4 cup coconut butter
- 1/4 cup carob powder
- 1/2 cup water
- 1/2 teaspoon ground vanilla beans or vanilla extract
- 4 drops peppermint essential oil
- 1/16 teaspoon salt

DIRECTIONS - CRUST

1. Process the almonds, coconut and salt in a food processor until the almonds are finely ground.
2. Add the dates and process until the mixture begins to stick together.
3. Press it into a 9" pie dish.

DIRECTIONS - FILLING

1. Combine the filling ingredients in a high speed blender until smooth.
2. Pour the filling into the crust.
3. Chill the pie at least 4 hours.
4. Enjoy!

Notes: Soak the dates for the filling while you prepare the crust.

Carob Mint Pie

Mango Coconut Fruit Tart

MANGO COCONUT FRUIT TART

Yield: 9" tart. Karen created the recipe for this delicious fruit tart as a birthday gift for herself. She described her idea for decorating it to her husband Scott, and went out to run some errands while it set. When she returned, Scott surprised her with this beautifully decorated treat.

INGREDIENTS - CRUST

- 1 cup unsweetened finely shredded dried coconut
- 1 cup almonds, preferably soaked and dehydrated
- 1/4 teaspoon salt
- 1/2 cup pecans, preferably soaked and dehydrated
- 1/2 cup pitted Medjool dates

INGREDIENTS - CUSTARD

- 2 cups coconut meat, from Young Thai coconut
- 1 large mango, peeled and pitted
- 1 tablespoon lime juice
- 1/16 teaspoon salt
- 2 pitted Medjool dates
- 1/2 teaspoon ground vanilla beans or vanilla extract
- 1/2 teaspoon sunflower lecithin
- 1 large mango, diced for topping
- 2 cups fruit, sliced for topping

DIRECTIONS - CRUST

1. Process the coconut, almonds and salt in a food processor until they are finely ground.
2. Add the pecans and process until they are coarsely chopped.
3. Add the dates and process until the mixture begins to stick together.
4. Press into a 9" tart pan.

DIRECTIONS - CUSTARD

1. Blend the coconut flesh, pulp of one mango, lime juice, salt, dates and vanilla in a high speed blender until smooth.
2. Add the sunflower lecithin and blend again until it is incorporated.
3. Spread the mixture into the crust.
4. Chill for 4 hours and top with diced mango and other fruit.

ORANGE CAROB PUDDING PIE

Yield: 9" pie - The raisins and the orange oil combine to give this pie a bright refreshing flavor.

INGREDIENTS - CRUST

- 1 cup finely shredded unsweetened dried coconut
- 1 cup almonds, preferably soaked and dehydrated
- 1/4 teaspoon salt
- 1 cup pitted Medjool dates

INGREDIENTS - FILLING

- 1/2 cup water
- 1/2 cup Irish Moss Paste (recipe in Chapter 7)
- 1 1/2 cups raisins, soaked
- 1/4 cup coconut butter
- 1/4 cup carob powder
- 1/2 teaspoon ground vanilla beans or vanilla extract
- 1/8 teaspoon orange oil
- 1/16 teaspoon salt

DIRECTIONS - CRUST

1. Process the coconut, almonds and salt in a food processor until the almonds are finely ground.
2. Add the dates and process until the mixture begins to stick together.
3. Press crust mixture into a 9" pie dish.

DIRECTIONS - FILLING

1. Combine the filling ingredients in a high speed blender until smooth.
2. Pour the filling mixture into the crust and chill at least 4 hours.

Orange Carob Pudding Pie

Peach Mango Pie

PEACH MANGO PIE

Yield: 9" pie - This is a very quick and delicious way to use those fresh summer peaches!

INGREDIENTS - CRUST

- 1 cup almonds, preferably soaked and dehydrated
- 1 cup finely shredded unsweetened dried coconut
- 1/4 teaspoon salt
- 1/2 cup pecans, preferably soaked and dehydrated
- 1/2 cup pitted Medjool dates

INGREDIENTS - FILLING

- 6 peaches
- 2 red or 3 yellow mangos
- 2 tablespoons lemon juice
- 1/16 teaspoon salt
- 4 pitted Medjool dates
- 1 tablespoon psyllium powder

DIRECTIONS - CRUST

1. Process the almonds, coconut and salt in a food processor until finely ground.
2. Add the pecans and process briefly until coarsely ground.
3. With the food processor running, add the dates and process until the mixture begins to stick together.

DIRECTIONS - FILLING

1. Dice the peaches and set them aside in a large bowl.
2. Blend the mangos, lemon juice, salt and dates in a high speed blender until smooth.
3. Add the psyllium and blend until it is incorporated.
4. Pour the mixture over the diced peaches and stir in the bowl.
5. Pour the mixture into the crust and chill for at least 4 hours.

STRAWBERRY BANANA COCONUT CREAM PIE

Yield: 9" pie - Are you looking for something to do with all of those summer berries? This is a simple, beautiful and delicious pie.

INGREDIENTS - CRUST

- 1 cup finely shredded unsweetened dried coconut
- 1 cup almonds, preferably soaked and dehydrated
- 1/4 teaspoon salt
- 1/2 cup pecans, preferably soaked and dehydrated
- 1/2 cup pitted Medjool dates

INGREDIENTS - TOPPING

- 1 cup strawberries, sliced
- 1 banana, sliced
- Shredded coconut as desired

INGREDIENTS - FILLING

- 2 bananas, sliced
- 1 banana
- 2 cups strawberries
- 1/2 cup coconut butter
- 4 pitted Medjool dates
- 1/2 teaspoon ground vanilla beans or vanilla extract
- 1/8 teaspoon salt
- 1 teaspoon sunflower lecithin

DIRECTIONS - CRUST

1. Process the coconut, almonds and salt in a food processor until finely ground.
2. Add the pecans and process just until they are coarsely chopped.
3. Add dates and process until the mixture begins to stick together.
4. Press the crust mixture into a glass pie dish.

DIRECTIONS - FILLING

1. Place the two sliced bananas in a medium bowl and set aside.
2. Put 1 banana, 2 cups of whole strawberries, the coconut butter, dates, vanilla and salt in a blender, and blend until smooth.
3. Add the lecithin and blend until it is incorporated.
4. Pour the mixture over the sliced bananas and stir well.
5. Spread the strawberry banana coconut filling in the pie crust.
6. Decorate the top with banana slices, strawberry slices and coconut flakes.
7. Chill at least 4 hours.

Strawberry Banana Coconut Cream Pie

Nut Free Pie Crusts

NUT FREE CRUSTS

Most, if not all of the raw pie crust recipes you'll find are nut heavy. We frequently get asked for recipes for nut free pie crusts by nut sensitive people and those who prefer to limit their intake of nuts for a variety of reasons. We've created two delicious ones, using shredded coconut, which is botanically a fruit, not a nut.

NUT FREE PIE CRUST

INGREDIENTS

- 1 1/2 cups finely shredded unsweetened dried coconut
- 1/2 cup lucuma powder
- 1/4 teaspoon salt
- 1/2 teaspoon ground vanilla beans or vanilla extract
- 1/2 cup raisins
- 1/2 cup pitted Medjool dates

DIRECTIONS

1. Process the first four ingredients in a food processor until combined.
2. Add the raisins and dates, and process until it sticks together.
3. Press into a 9" pie pan or tart pan or spring form pan.
4. Chill, or fill and chill.

SIMPLE NUT FREE PIE CRUST

INGREDIENTS

- 2 cups finely shredded unsweetened dried coconut
- 1/4 teaspoon salt
- 1/2 teaspoon ground vanilla beans or vanilla extract
- 3/4 cup pitted Medjool dates

DIRECTIONS

1. Process all ingredients in a food processor until the mixture begins to stick together.
2. Add a few more dates if needed to make the mixture stick together.
3. Press into a 9" pie pan or tart pan or spring form pan.
4. Chill or fill and chill.

Notes: Dates are a natural product and vary in moisture content and stickiness, so you may need to add more dates if the mixture is not sticking together.

CHAPTER 3

Cakes

Cheesecake

Layer Cake

German Carob Cake

CHEESECAKE

Yield: 8" round - With only 1/2 cup of macadamia nuts in the filling, this is a light cheese cake.

INGREDIENTS - CRUST

- 1/2 cup almonds, preferably soaked and dehydrated
- 1/4 cup finely shredded unsweetened dried coconut
- 1/16 teaspoon salt
- 1/4 cup walnuts, preferably soaked and dehydrated
- 2 teaspoons lucuma powder
- 5 Turkish apricots, dried
- 2 pitted Medjool dates

INGREDIENTS - FILLING

- 2 cups peeled zucchini, about 8 oz. (cut into 1/4" rounds to measure)
- 1 1/2 cups pitted Medjool dates, packed
- 3 tablespoon lemon juice
- 1/2 cup coconut butter
- 2 tablespoons vanilla extract
- 1/4 teaspoon salt
- 1/4 cup Irish Moss Paste (recipe in Chapter 7
- 1/2 cup macadamia nuts
- 1 teaspoon sunflower lecithin

DIRECTIONS - CRUST

1. Process the almonds, coconut and salt until finely ground.
2. Add the walnuts and lucuma powder and process until it is incorporated.
3. Slice the apricots and dates in half and drop them into the food processor while it is running.
4. Continue processing until the mixture just begins to stick together.
5. Press it into an 8" spring form pan.

DIRECTIONS - FILLING

1. Puree the zucchini in a high speed blender.
2. Add the dates and lemon juice and blend until smooth.
3. Add the coconut butter, vanilla, salt, Irish moss paste and macadamia nuts, and blend until smooth.
4. Add the sunflower lecithin and blend until it is incorporated.
5. Pour the filling mixture on top of the crust in the springform pan.
6. Chill the cheesecake for at least 4 hours.
7. Slice, serve and enjoy.

Notes: This is great topped with Strawberry Coulis (Chapter 5), and fresh strawberries. Double the filling recipe for a taller cake.

Cheesecake

Layer Cake

LAYER CAKE

Yield: Yield: 8" round cake. This layer cake is perfect for birthdays and celebrations and can be beautifully decorated using a pastry bag and decorative tips.

INGREDIENTS

- 5 cups finely shredded unsweetened dried coconut
- 3 cups of walnuts, preferably soaked and dehydrated
- 1/2 teaspoon salt
- 1 tablespoon psyllium powder
- 4 teaspoons ground vanilla beans or vanilla extract
- 32 large, pitted Medjool dates
- 1 cup lucuma powder (or 1/2 cup lucuma & 1/2 cup carob powder for carob cake)
- 2 peeled zucchini, shredded
- 1 recipe Carob Cashew Frosting (recipe in Chapter 7)

DIRECTIONS

1. Process the coconut, walnuts, salt, psyllium and vanilla in a food processor until the almonds are finely ground.
2. Add the dates and process just until the mixture begins to stick together.
3. Add the lucuma powder and process until it is incorporated.
4. Add shredded zucchini and pulse just until it is mixed in.
5. Gently press half of the dough into an 8" round spring-form pan, being careful not to pack it tightly. Place a parchment round on top, and gently press the other half of the dough on top of the parchment paper.
6. Chill for at least 4 hours.
7. Remove the cake from the pan and separate it into two layers removing the middle parchment round.
8. Frost with carob cashew frosting.

Notes: This recipe makes a "yellow" cake. Replace 1/2 cup of the lucuma powder with 1/2 cup of carob powder for a carob cake. You can also make half of the recipe in two 4" springform pans for a cute 4" cake or gently press it into a 6" round cake pan for a single layer cake.

GERMAN CAROB CAKE

Yield: 8" round cake. This is a deliciously healthy version of German Chocolate Cake!

INGREDIENTS

- 5 cups finely shredded unsweetened dried coconut
- 3 cups walnuts, preferably soaked and dehydrated
- 1/2 teaspoon salt
- 1 tablespoon psyllium powder
- 4 teaspoons ground vanilla beans or vanilla extract
- 32 large pitted Medjool dates
- 1/2 cup lucuma powder
- 1/2 cup carob powder
- 3 tablespoons maca powder
- 2 peeled zucchini, shredded
- 1 recipe Coconut Pecan Frosting (recipe in Chapter 7)

DIRECTIONS

1. Process the coconut, walnuts, salt, psyllium, and vanilla in a food processor until the almonds are finely ground.
2. Add the dates and process until the mixture just begins to stick together.
3. Add the lucuma powder, the carob powder and the maca powder and process until incorporated.
4. Add the shredded zucchini and pulse just until it is mixed in.
5. Gently press half of the dough into an 8" round spring-form pan, being careful not to pack it tightly. Place a parchment round on top, and gently press the other half of the dough on top of the parchment paper
6. Chill for at least 2 hours.
7. Remove the cake from the pan and separate it into two layers removing the middle parchment round.
8. Frost with Coconut Pecan Frosting (recipe in Chapter 7).

German Carob Cake

CHAPTER 4

Candy

Carob Crispy Candy

Low Glycemic Superfood Peppermint Thins

Marzipan

Pomegranate Candy

Amaretto Truffles

CAROB CRISPY CANDY

Yield: 12 pieces - These are delicious and so quick and easy to make. Just keep some dehydrated buckwheat in your freezer, and you can whip these up any time.

INGREDIENTS

- 4 tablespoons coconut butter
- 2 tablespoons coconut nectar
- 2 tablespoons almond butter
- 1/16 teaspoon salt (a pinch)
- 1/4 teaspoon ground vanilla beans or vanilla extract
- 2 teaspoons carob powder
- 2 - 4 tablespoons of buckwheat, sprouted and dehydrated (See instructions in Chapter 7)

DIRECTIONS

1. In a bowl, stir together the coconut butter, coconut nectar and almond butter until smooth.
2. Add the salt and vanilla and stir until they are incorporated.
3. Add the carob powder and stir until smooth.
4. Add the buckwheat and stir until evenly distributed.
5. Line a mini-muffin pan with paper baking cups.
6. Fill each one with 2 teaspoons of the mixture.
7. Chill the candy for at least one hour.
8. Enjoy!

Notes: Add one or two drops of peppermint essential oil for a carob mint candy, add a teaspoon of maca powder for a carob malt candy or add one or two drops of orange essential oil for carob orange candy. It is fun to create a "bridge mix" by making all four and combining them on a plate when serving.

Carob Crispy Candy

Low Glycemic Superfood Peppermint Thins

LOW GLYCEMIC SUPERFOOD PEPPERMINT THINS

Yield: 8"x8" pan. High in omega 3 fats from the hemp seeds, selenium from the Brazil nuts, chlorophyll from the greens and antiviral lauric acid from the coconut, these treats are much better for you than the peppermint patties you may have eaten before.

INGREDIENTS

- 1/2 cup hemp seeds
- 1 cup finely shredded unsweetened dried coconut
- 1/4 teaspoon green stevia powder
- 4 drops peppermint essential oil
- 1 teaspoon chlorella powder
- 1/8 teaspoon ground vanilla beans or vanilla extract
- 1/8 cup Brazil nuts
- 1/8 teaspoon salt

DIRECTIONS

1. Process all the ingredients in a food processor until almost smooth.
2. Spread the mixture thin on a wax paper or parchment paper lined tray, and score* into desired sizes.
3. Freeze for at least half an hour.

Notes: These very low glycemic treats contain no sweeteners. If you prefer the filling a little bit sweeter, you can add 1/4 cup pitted dates. They are very refreshing eaten right from the freezer.

* To score, make shallow cuts in the surface of the batter so that it will easily break apart into the desired size and shape when dry. It works best to press down through the mixture with a pizza rocker, but a knife can be used as well.

MARZIPAN

Yield: Sixty 1/2" x 1 1/2 " candies - These are delicious eaten right out of the freezer!

INGREDIENTS

- 1 1/2 cups unsweetened finely shredded dried coconut
- 1 cup macadamia nuts
- 1 cup pitted Medjool dates
- 1/2 teaspoon almond extract, pure, organic
- 1/8 teaspoon salt

DIRECTIONS

1. Process 1 cup of the coconut and all of the other ingredients in the food processor until smooth.
2. Stir in the remaining coconut.
3. Spread the mixture 1/4 inch thick on a wax paper or parchment paper lined baking dish.
4. Freeze it until firm.
5. Score* and cut it into snack sized pieces.
6. Store them in zip lock bags or an airtight container in the freezer for a quick pick-me-up.

Notes: These are also good rolled into 1 inch balls.

* To score, make shallow cuts in the surface of the batter so that it will easily break apart into the desired size and shape when dry. It works best to press down through the mixture with a pizza rocker, but a knife can be used as well.

Marzipan

Pomegranate Candy

POMEGRANATE CANDY

Yield: 24 – Simply sweet and tart.

INGREDIENTS

- 1 cup finely shredded unsweetened dried coconut
- 1 cup macadamia nuts
- 1/2 cup pomegranate powder

DIRECTIONS

1. Process all three ingredients in a food processor until combined into a paste.
2. Press the paste into candy molds.
3. Freeze for 4 hours.
4. Pop them out of the molds and enjoy.
5. Store in an airtight container in the freezer.

AMARETTO TRUFFLES

Yield: 48. These are a perfect ending after
an Italian meal.

INGREDIENTS

- 1/4 cup almond butter
- 1/4 cup coconut butter
- 1/4 cup lucuma powder
- 1/4 cup carob powder
- 1/8 teaspoon salt
- 2 teaspoons ground vanilla beans or vanilla extract
- 1 tablespoon almond extract
- 1/2 cup date paste (recipe in Chapter 7)
- 1/2 cup almonds, ground to a powder

DIRECTIONS

1. Combine all ingredients except the ground almonds.
2. Process in a food processor or stir together until smooth.
3. Form a teaspoon of dough into a ball. Continue forming balls until all dough is used.
4. Roll balls in ground almonds.
5. Freeze for at least 1/2 hr.
6. Store in the freezer in an air tight container.

Amaretto Truffles

CHAPTER 5

Frozen Concoctions

Carob Mint Smoothie

Mango Coconut Mint "Ice Cream"

Raspberry Sorbet

Banana "Ice Cream" with Strawberry Coulis

CAROB MINT SMOOTHIE

Yield: 4 cups - Sometimes you just feel like having a light, refreshing dessert, and this frosty treat is just that.

INGREDIENTS

- 1/2 cup water
- 4 tablespoons hemp seeds
- 6 pitted Medjool dates
- 3 tablespoons carob powder
- 10 - 20 peppermint or spearmint leaves
- 4 cups spinach
- 3 cups ice

DIRECTIONS

1. Blend the water, hemp seeds, dates, carob powder, and mint until smooth.
2. Add the spinach and blend until smooth.
3. Add 3 cups of crushed ice and blend just until the mixture is thick and frosty.

Notes: 1 Tablespoon of dried mint can be substituted for the fresh mint leaves. More mint leaves can be used for a stronger mint flavor. You can even make ice cream by blending in more ice to make it thicker.

Carob Mint Smoothie

Mango Coconut Mint "Ice Cream"

MANGO COCONUT MINT "ICE CREAM"

Yield: 2 cups - This recipe came about as a result of Karen and Linda Marie Graziano, MBA, Coach and Chef, brainstorming about a dessert to teach in a class with an Asian theme.

INGREDIENTS

- 1/2 cup coconut water, from a young Thai coconut
- 1/4 cup coconut meat, from a young Thai coconut
- 2 pitted Medjool dates
- 10 ounces frozen mango
- 1 tablespoon of fresh peppermint leaves or 1 teaspoon of dried peppermint leaves

DIRECTIONS

1. Blend the coconut water, coconut meat and dates in a high speed blender until smooth.
2. Add the mint and frozen mango and blend just until smooth.
3. Enjoy!

RASPBERRY SORBET

Yield: 3-4 servings. This is a quick delicious sorbet that can be made with any kind of frozen fruit that you desire.

INGREDIENTS

- 1/2 cup nut milk (Chapter 7)
- 2 pitted Medjool dates
- 10 ounces frozen raspberries

DIRECTIONS

1. Blend the nut milk and the dates in a high speed blender until smooth.
2. Add the frozen fruit and blend again until smooth.
3. Serve and Enjoy!

Notes:

- Water may be used in place of the nut milk. The sorbet will just be a little less creamy.
- Sorbet can also be made by running the frozen fruit through a juicer.

Raspberry Sorbet

Banana "Ice Cream" with Strawberry Coulis

BANANA "ICE CREAM" WITH STRAWBERRY COULIS

Yield: 6 servings. This is a very quick and easy dessert. The Strawberry Coulis can be stored in refrigerator up to a week and used as a handy topping on cheese cake or other desserts.

INGREDIENTS

- 12 frozen bananas
- 20 ounces strawberries, fresh or frozen
- 4 pitted Medjool dates
- 1/2 tablespoon lemon juice
- 1/2 teaspoon psyllium powder

DIRECTIONS

1. Blend the strawberries, dates and lemon juice until smooth.
2. Add the psyllium and blend until incorporated.
3. In a Champion or Green Star Juicer, run the bananas through with the blank plate in place. The Omega juicer and even a hand cranked wheat grass juicer work well, too. Alternatively, place the bananas in your food processor and process until creamy. Serve immediately.

CHAPTER 6

Other Fun Foods

Blueberry Muffins, Scones or Bread

Coconut Pudding Parfait

Doughnut Holes

Carrot Raisin Bread

Blueberry Muffins, Scones or Bread

BLUEBERRY MUFFINS, SCONES OR BREAD

Yield: 12 slices

INGREDIENTS

- 1 cup buckwheat, soaked and sprouted (See instructions in Chapter 7)
- 4 pitted Medjool dates
- 1/4 teaspoon salt
- 1/2 teaspoon ground vanilla beans or vanilla extract
- 1/2 cup flax seeds, ground
- 1 tablespoon psyllium powder
- 1/2 - 1 cup of fresh blueberries

DIRECTIONS

1. Combine the buckwheat, dates, salt and vanilla in a food processor, and process until the mixture is smooth.
2. Add the flax seeds and process until combined.
3. Add the psyllium and process until it is incorporated.
4. Gently fold in the blueberries.
5. Form the dough into a loaf on a cutting board.
6. Slice the dough into 12 pieces.
7. Place the slices on a mesh screen on a dehydrator tray.
8. Dehydrate the slices at 105° F for 8 hours.
9. Serve warm.

Notes: You can also line a loaf pan with plastic wrap or parchment paper, and fill it as a mold. Turn it over on the cutting board to release the mixture, and then slice. You can also drop the dough onto the mesh screen in the shape of a scone. This recipe works best with fresh fruit. The liquid from thawed frozen fruit will gum up the dough and cause the bread to be too dense.

COCONUT PUDDING PARFAIT

Yield: 4 servings

INGREDIENTS

- 2 young Thai coconuts
- 1/2 cup pitted Medjool dates
- 1 teaspoon ground vanilla beans or vanilla extract
- 1/16 teaspoon salt
- 1/4 cup carob powder

DIRECTIONS

1. Open the coconuts (There are many You Tube videos on how to do this).
2. Reserve the liquid, scoop out the meat, and put the meat into your blender.
3. Add 3/8 cup of dates, 1/2 cup of the reserved coconut water, vanilla and salt.
4. Blend until it is creamy and smooth.
5. Add extra liquid if needed.
6. Spoon 1/2 of the pudding into a bowl.
7. To the remaining pudding in the blender, add the carob powder, remaining dates and about 1/4 cup of the coconut water.
8. Blend the mixture until it is smooth and creamy. If it is too thick, add extra coconut water to desired consistency.
9. Into a glass dessert dish or small wine glass, spoon 1 - 2 tablespoons of carob pudding, then 2 tablespoons of vanilla pudding and then another 1 - 2 tablespoons of carob pudding.
10. Top with a cherry or berry and serve.

Coconut Pudding Parfait

Doughnut Holes

DOUGHNUT HOLES

Yield: 3 dozen - This is really a fun recipe to make and to eat, and they make your house smell like a bakery while they are dehydrating.

INGREDIENTS

- 2 cups finely shredded unsweetened dried coconut
- 1 cup date paste (recipe in Chapter 7)
- 1/4 teaspoon salt
- 1 teaspoon ground vanilla beans or vanilla extract
- 1/2 cup lucuma powder
- 1/2 cup flax seeds, ground
- 2 teaspoons psyllium
- 2 tablespoons lucuma powder, for rolling
- 1 tablespoon carob powder, for rolling
- 1/4 teaspoon cinnamon, for rolling

DIRECTIONS

1. Combine the coconut, date paste (recipe in Chapter 7), salt, vanilla and 1/2 cup of lucuma powder in a food processor.
2. Add the flax seeds and process until well combined.
3. Add the psyllium and process until it is incorporated.
4. Roll one tablespoon of dough into a ball. Continue rolling by the tablespoonful until all of the dough is used.
5. Combine on a small plate or bowl 1 tablespoon of lucuma powder with 1/4 teaspoon of cinnamon.
6. Put 1 tablespoon of carob powder on another small plate or bowl, and 1 tablespoon of lucuma powder on another small plate or bowl.
7. Roll one dozen balls in the carob powder, and place them on a mesh screen on a dehydrator tray.
8. Roll one dozen balls in the lucuma powder, and place them on a mesh screen on a dehydrator tray.
9. Roll one dozen balls in the lucuma powder and cinnamon mixture, and place them on a mesh screen on a dehydrator tray.
10. Dehydrate the balls at 105° F 12-14 hours. Enjoy!

CARROT RAISIN BREAD

Yield: One large loaf or several small loaves. This is a great comfort food packed with nutrition.

INGREDIENTS

- 4 cups carrot pulp
- 1 cup date paste (recipe in Chapter 7)
- 1/2 teaspoon cinnamon
- 1/4 teaspoon cloves
- 1/4 teaspoon salt
- 1/4 teaspoon ginger powder
- 1/2 teaspoon ground vanilla beans or vanilla extract
- 1 cup flax seeds, ground
- 1 teaspoon psyllium powder
- 1 cup raisins

DIRECTIONS

1. Knead all of the ingredients except the raisins, psyllium powder and flax in large bowl.
2. Add the ground flax seeds and knead until well mixed.
3. Add the psyllium and knead until mixed.
4. Add the raisins and knead until mixed.
5. Shape the mixture into a loaf, or press it into lined loaf pans and remove.
6. Slice the loaf.
7. Lay the slices on mesh dehydrator sheets.
8. Dehydrate the slices at 135° F for 45 minutes.
9. Turn the dehydrator down to 105° F and continue dehydrating 8 - 12 hours until firm.

Notes: The thicker the slices are, the longer they will take to dehydrate.

Carrot Raisin Bread

CHAPTER 7

Toppings & Components

Sprouted Buckwheat

Date Paste

Irish Moss Paste

Nut Milk

Marshmallow Topping

Carob Topping

Caramel Topping

Vanilla Custard

Blueberry Jam

Coconut Pecan Frosting

Carob Cashew Frosting

SPROUTED BUCKWHEAT

INGREDIENTS

- Raw buckwheat with the black hulls removed
- Water 4:1 ratio of water to buckwheat

DIRECTIONS

1. Place buckwheat in a bowl
2. Cover with water, with a 4:1 ratio of water to buckwheat
3. Allow to soak overnight. Be sure the bowl has extra room in it as the buckwheat expands.
4. The next day, rinse the buckwheat and place in a strainer.
5. Rinse twice a day until the buckwheat has sprouted and the sprouts are less than half the length of the seed.
6. Set buckwheat aside to drain while preparing the other ingredients.

Notes: Sprouted buckwheat can be used to make cereal, breads, pizza crusts, crackers and cookies.

DATE PASTE

Many recipes that use liquid sweetener can be made with date paste instead. It's easy to make and keeps in the refrigerator for at least a week, if not longer.

INGREDIENTS

- 1 cup dates, pitted
- 1/2 cup water

DIRECTIONS

1. Blend ingredients in a high speed blender until smooth.

ALTERNATIVE

1. Cover the dates with water, and let them soak for 20 minutes. Then, process the dates with 1/2 cup of the soak water in the food processor until smooth.

IRISH MOSS PASTE

INGREDIENTS

- 1/2 cup dry Irish moss
- 1/2 cup water
- Additional water (For soaking)

DIRECTIONS

1. Rinse 1/2 cup of Irish moss.
2. Soak it for 3 to 8 hours, and rinse it again.
3. It will expand to about one cup.
4. Make sure to rinse away all of the sand and salt.
5. Put the Irish moss in a high speed blender with 1/2 cup of water.
6. Blend until it is smooth.
7. Refrigerate the paste for 2 hours to let it set.

Notes: Irish moss paste will last in the refrigerator for 10 days in a glass jar with an air tight lid. You can also freeze in ice cube trays for months.

PREPARING NUTS AND SEEDS FOR RECIPES

Nuts and seeds are easier to digest and more nutritious if you activate them first. When you cover them in water and let them soak, the germination process begins. The enzyme inhibitors, which keep the nut or seed from sprouting, are deactivated and the proteins and fats begin to break down into smaller molecules. The nuts and seeds are then easier to digest.

To Activate Nuts and Seeds: Place them in a glass jar or ceramic bowl or in a colander in a bowl, and completely cover them with enough water to allow for doubling in size. Soak on kitchen counter or in the refrigerator for 4 hours or up to 8 hours. Harder nuts like almonds and hazelnuts require longer soaking time while softer and more delicate nuts and seeds require less time. Rinse and drain.

You can use them immediately, or you can leave them in the strainer and allow them to begin to sprout. Sunflower seeds sprout in 4-6 hours. Almonds don't fully sprout, but develop a short tail. Macadamia nuts don't sprout at all. They turn mushy if left in water too long. It's less important to soak the nuts that don't have skins, like macadamia nuts and cashews. In fact, soaking either of these for too long causes them to get really mushy and lose their taste.

Activated nuts can be stored in the refrigerator for up to 4 days. After that, they begin to get moldy. If you have a dehydrator, you can dehydrate the activated nuts for a couple of days, then store in the freezer. This way, you can just use what you need without having to soak in advance.

Some people soak a pound or two of nuts for 4-8 hours then dehydrate so they always have a handy supply of activated nuts.

NUT MILK

INGREDIENTS

- 3 cups filtered water
- 1/2 cups nuts, soaked 8 - 12 hours*

DIRECTIONS

1. Drain the nuts, and rinse them until the water runs clear.
2. Combine the nuts and the water in a high speed blender until you hear the nuts stop grinding, taking care not to over-blend because the finer you blend the harder it is to squeeze out of the bag since the fibers clog up the fine mesh holes.
3. Line a pitcher with a nut milk bag.
4. Pour the mixture into the nut milk bag. **
5. Strain the liquid into the pitcher.
6. Squeeze the nut milk bag as if milking a cow to get all the liquid out.
7. Save the pulp in the freezer for making cakes and breads.

NOTES

- *White nuts, such as cashews and macadamia nuts, do not need to be soaked before following this procedure.
- *Add more nuts for a thicker milk.
- ** Nut milk bags are available online. You can also use a paint straining bag, available at most home improvement stores.

MARSHMALLOW TOPPING

INGREDIENTS

- 1 cup 1/4" round slices of peeled zucchini
- 1/2 teaspoon vanilla extract
- 1 cup coconut meat from young Thai coconut
- 1/4 cup macadamia nuts
- 2 teaspoons psyllium powder

DIRECTIONS

1. Blend the zucchini, 1/2 teaspoon vanilla extract and the coconut meat in a high speed blender until smooth.
2. Add the macadamia nuts and blend until smooth.
3. Add the psyllium powder and blend until the mixture thickens.
4. Put the mixture in a pastry bag and pipe on top of your favorite dessert.

CAROB TOPPING

INGREDIENTS

- 1/4 cup coconut butter
- 1/4 cup coconut nectar
- 1/2 cup carob powder
- 1/4 cup water

DIRECTIONS

1. Blend the coconut butter, coconut nectar, carob powder and water in a high speed blender - on low speed until combined.
2. Put the mixture in a pastry bag and pipe on top of your favorite dessert.

Marshmallow & Carob Toppings

CARAMEL TOPPING

INGREDIENTS

- 1/2 cup cashews, soaked 20 minutes
- 1 cup pitted Medjool dates, soaked 20 minutes (retain soak water)
- 1/2 teaspoon vanilla extract
- 1/4 teaspoon salt
- 1/2 cup date soak water
- 1/2 teaspoon sunflower lecithin

DIRECTIONS

1. Blend the cashews, dates, vanilla extract, 1/4 teaspoon salt and the date soak water in a high speed blender until smooth.
2. Add the sunflower lecithin and blend again until incorporated.
3. Put the mixture in a pastry bag and chill for at least 2 hours.
4. Pipe on top of brownies, cake or other dessert.

VANILLA CUSTARD

Yield: 1 serving. This recipe works well as is for filling or topping for another dessert. To make as a standalone dessert, triple the recipe and add extra dates to desired sweetness.

INGREDIENTS

- 1 cup coconut meat from young Thai coconut
- 1/4 cup purified water
- 1 Medjool date, pitted
- 1/2 teaspoon ground vanilla beans or vanilla extract
- 1 smidgeon salt (1/32 teaspoon)
- 1/4 teaspoon sunflower lecithin

DIRECTIONS

1. Blend the coconut meat, water, date, vanilla and 1/32 teaspoon (smidgeon) of salt in a high speed blender until smooth.
2. Add the sunflower lecithin, and blend until it is incorporated.

BLUEBERRY JAM

INGREDIENTS

- 1 cup fresh blueberries
- 2 tablespoons lemon juice
- 2 pitted Medjool dates
- 1/2 teaspoon psyllium powder

DIRECTIONS

1. Combine the blueberries, lemon juice and dates in a high speed blender until smooth.
2. Add the psyllium and blend until it is incorporated and the mixture begins to thicken.

Notes: If blueberries are out of season, use 1 cup of frozen blueberries with 3 dates and 3/4 teaspoon of psyllium.

COCONUT PECAN FROSTING

Yield: 3 cups.

INGREDIENTS

- 1 1/2 cups water
- 3 cups pitted Medjool dates
- 1/8 teaspoon salt
- 2 teaspoons ground vanilla beans or vanilla extract
- 1 cup finely shredded unsweetened dried coconut
- 3/4 cup pecans, finely chopped

DIRECTIONS

1. Blend the water and the dates in a high speed blender until smooth.
2. Add the salt and the vanilla and blend again.
3. Put mixture in a bowl and stir in the coconut and pecans.

Coconut Pecan Frosting

CAROB CASHEW FROSTING

Yield: 3 cups

INGREDIENTS

- 1 cup of cashews, soaked 20 minutes
- 2 cups pitted Medjool dates, soaked for 20 minutes
- 1 teaspoon vanilla extract
- 1/2 teaspoon salt
- 1/2 cup date soak water
- 1/4 cup coconut butter
- 1/2 cup carob powder
- 1 teaspoon sunflower lecithin

DIRECTIONS

1. Blend all of the ingredients except the carob powder and sunflower lecithin until smooth.
2. Add the carob powder and blend until smooth.
3. Add the lecithin and blend until totally incorporated.
4. Put the mixture in a bowl and chill for at least 4 hours.

Notes: Macadamia nuts may be used in place of cashews.

ABOUT THE AUTHORS

Dr. Ritamarie Loscalzo, MS, DC, CCN, DACBN

Dr. Ritamarie's transformational journey from exhausted to energized inspires women of all ages to find vibrant health and build a great life.

From a chronically fatigued and sick twenty-something to over 50 and fabulous, Dr Ritamarie Loscalzo combines over 25 years of vibrant living with the latest scientific health knowledge to educate, inspire and coach you on your journey to vibrant health.

Passionate about fresh, whole, green foods, low stress living and a dash of daily fun, Dr Ritamarie focuses on simple effective ways to motivate you to achieve your health goals.

A Chiropractic Doctor, Certified in Acupuncture, Nutrition and Herbal Medicine, as well as a certified living foods chef, instructor, coach, speaker and author, Dr Ritamarie specializes in women's fatigue, hormone issues, digestive challenges and immune rebalancing. She practices integrative health care, using her knowledge of biochemistry, nutrition, herbs, structural alignment and the power of the mind to return the body to a state of natural, vibrant health. Dr. Ritamarie incorporates ancient healing wisdom with modern functional medicine to gently awaken your inner healer.

Dr. Ritamarie provides the ingredients for good health through her coaching practice, seminars, workshops, and books, guiding countless individuals to better health through diet. She is available for in-person and long-distance consultations and coaching and as a speaker for your next conference.

ABOUT THE AUTHORS

Chef Karen Osborne

Karen Osborne, a lifetime active pianist, has been preparing gourmet raw food since being introduced to it in 2001.

Karen's body became her new, finely tuned instrument after experiencing the energy and great health that followed the elimination of gluten, dairy and refined sugar from her diet and adding lots of greens.

Karen's passionate performances now are focused on creating raw food experiences as treats of harmonic sensations, developing flavors like a symphony. From delicate to dynamic, her food is music to the palate.

Specializing in tantalizing raw versions of favorites like Tiramisu, she loves to help people with the food part of their transition to a healthy lifestyle that also includes exercise, sun and sleep.

Karen is a graduate of Living Light Culinary Arts Institute and sells her creations in the Austin, TX area where she gives private instruction in Raw Food preparation, demonstrates Raw Food Joy regularly for a market in South Austin, manages Dr. Ritamarie's Co-op and teaches classes. www.karenorawchef.com

OUR OTHER HEALTH & NUTRITION BOOKS & PROGRAMS

Dried and Gone to Heaven e-book The only book of its kind. It's the most complete and up to date information about how to use your food dehydrator to create mouth watering comfort foods without health-compromising ingredients like gluten, dairy, sugar and processed and heated oils. All recipes are 100% plant based and all ingredients are uncooked.
http://www.DriedAndGoneToHeaven.com

Dried and Gone to Heaven DVD Home Study Kit Full instruction on the care and use of your dehydrator, health gems and complete recipe demonstrations so you can make all your favorite comfort foods in ways that support your health rather than drain it. Complete with DVDs, recipe guide and instruction manual, laminated reference cards and a whole new perspective on life.
http://www.DriedAndGoneToHeaven.com

The Secret of Being Sexy and Vibrant at Any Age By sexy we mean glowing from the inside out so that you radiate health and vibrance and attract attention because of your inner and outer beauty. Learn the secrets of balancing your hormones and keeping them safe so you can regain your youthful vim and vigor and be healthy and vibrant no matter what your age. http://www.vibranthormones.com

Balance My Body Blueprint Balancing body chemistry and hormones through diet, lifestyle and nutritional supplementation - a four month journey of self discovery and healing.
http://www.BalanceMyBodyBlueprint.com

Eat Your Way Out of Pain An interactive course with over 2 hours of audio, a recipe guide, transcripts and bonuses to support you in eating in a manner that decreases pain and inflammation and leaves you feeling comfortable and energized. Free sample recipes and anti-inflammatory food chart.
http://www.EatYourWayOutOfPain.com

Six Week Deep Tissue Detox A guided journey through the detoxification process. Clean out your digestive tract, heal your leaky gut and enhance liver detoxification. http://www.sixweekdetox.com

The Vibrant Health Mindset Success System Get out of your own way. Get in touch with your core values, set bold health goals and be guided step by step through creating and managing a detailed plan. Learn valuable strategies for managing emotional eating, making consistently healthy choices and staying true to your true self. No more self sabotage, starting over and self reproach.
http://www.VibrantHealthMindset.com

Get Your Gut In Gear This is a unique program that guides you step by step through restoring balance to your digestive tract so you can experience more energy, a flat happy belly and increased mental clarity. http://www.getyourgutingear.com

Green Cleanse Program This is a simple 7 day cleanse that is easy to do and results in profound bodily transformation. Pounds melt away, skin clears and mood, energy and focus soar.
http://www.greensmoothiecleanse.com

Ageless Woman Audio recordings from 3 nights of focused ageless health information for women. Learn how to balance your hormones and sail gracefully through your transition years ...and it's best to start long BEFORE menopause begins. http://www.drritamarie.com/go/AgelessWoman

Transforming Stress Audio, workbook, and transcript of a 90 minute live teleclass that guides you gently through a process of transforming your typical health-depleting reaction to day-to-day stress into a powerful experience that creates inner balance and improved health.
http://www.drritamarie.com/shop/home-study

Get Your Green On Live video recordings of a daylong class on the art of making delicious greens to power charge your nutrition and create vibrant energy. Includes video demonstrations of sprouting, juicing, sea vegetables, and making delicious GREEN recipes.
http://www.drritamarie.com/GreensClass.php

Power Breakfast Ideas Quick, healthy and energizing recipes and tips for starting your morning with recipes that give you plenty of energy to fuel you through the day!
http://www.rawpowerbreakfast.com

Quick Lunch & Dinner Ideas for Healthy Meals on the Run A valuable resource of more than just recipes! A complete guide to creating quick and delicious meals from ingredients you have on hand.
http://drritamarie.com/classes/lunchdinner.htm

Quick & Easy Hearty Soups Warm, nourishing and deeply satisfying recipes for soups brimming with living food goodness. http://drritamarie.com/classes/soup.htm

Online Video Classes Include access to a private web page that includes a pdf format recipe e-book with photos of each recipe, and a separate video for each recipe.

Amazing Gluten Free Bread - the Ultimate Comfort Food Turned Health Food Online Video There's no need to feel deprived. With a little creativity and advance planning, you can enjoy mouthwatering sandwiches, bread and pizza brimming with nutritious goodness. http://www.drritamarie.com/videoclasses/breadmaking2010-08

Thai Food Goes Raw Online Video Gluten free, dairy free and brimming with exotic spices, these recipes are easy to make and will delight any palate. http://www.drritamarie.com/videoclasses/thaigoesraw

Gluten Free Pizza and Pasta Online Video Experience the traditional tastes of Italy with a gluten free and dairy free twist as we prepare pizza (crust, sauce and cheese), Living Lasagna, Rawvioli, Manicotti, Spaghetti and other pasta dishes, "Parmesan Cheese" and more. http://drritamarie.com/videoclasses/pizza2010-10

Healthy Holiday Feasts Online Video It's easy to prepare a delicious, nutritious, gluten free, dairy free holiday meal that everyone can enjoy! http://drritamarie.com/videoclasses/holidayfeasts2010-11

Sweets for the Holidays Amazing gluten free, dairy free, raw vegan versions of traditional holiday treats such as gingerbread men, cookies in festive seasonal shapes, candy, turtle brownies and more. http://drritamarie.com/videoclasses/holidaysweets2010-12

Seasonal Specials Halloween, Thanksgiving, Christmas and Hanukkah recipe books and videos. http://www.drritamarie.com/shop/seasonal

Private Health Consultations, Kitchen Set-Up, Shopping Assistance http://www.drritamarie.com/shop/coaching-programs

21059400R00064

Made in the USA
Charleston, SC
03 August 2013